DANNY HARF

WAKEBOARDING SUPERSTAR

CHRISTOPHER D. GORANSON

rosen
central™

The Rosen Publishing Group, Inc., New York

To Lindsay, whose adventurous spirit is always inspiring

Published in 2005 by The Rosen Publishing Group, Inc.
29 East 21st Street, New York, NY 10010

First Edition

Library of Congress Cataloging-in-Publication Data

Goranson, Christopher D.
Danny Harf: wakeboarding superstar / by Christopher D. Goranson.— 1st ed.
    p. cm. — (Extreme sports biographies)
Summary: Profiles Danny Harf, a Southern California native and a wakeboarding champion, focusing on the tricks and stunts he performs at the X Games and other competitions.
Includes bibliographical references and index.
ISBN 1-4042-0066-5 (lib. bdg.)
1. Harf, Danny—Juvenile literature. 2. Wakeboarders—California—Biography—Juvenile literature. [1. Harf, Danny. 2. Wakeboarders.]
I. Title. II. Series: Extreme sports biographies (Rosen Publishing Group)
GV838.H364G67 2005
797.3'2'092–dc22

                                                              2003022257

Manufactured in the United States of America

On the cover: Left: Danny Harf in action at the August 2002 ESPN X Games competition in Philadelphia, Pennsylvania. Right: Danny Harf poses for a portrait during the August 2003 Vans Triple Crown of Wakeboarding competition in Indianapolis, Indiana.

CONTENTS

Wakeboarding, a combination of surfing, snowboarding, and waterskiing, is today's fastest-growing water sport. It attracts both amateurs and professionals from around the world. According to the World Wakeboard Association, nearly 2.7 million people participate in wakeboarding worldwide.

Danny Harf, a twenty-one-year-old professional wakeboarder, is a sport favorite. At only sixteen years of age at the 2001 X Games VII, Harf won the gold medal with a crazy set of tricks, including an off-axis 540 followed in his second pass by a huge 900. With a quick launch into the professional ranks, the sky is the limit as Harf continues his creative riding style.

In 2003, Harf added a national championship to his three prior X Games wins. As the first rider in the WWA Wakeboard National Pro Men's Final, Harf wowed the crowd with a heelside 720 followed by a toeside 900. Experts called the run one of the best in the history of the sport.

In this book, we'll examine what it takes to become a professional wakeboarder like Harf and what separates his abilities from the rest of the pack. Whether you're a beginner

Danny Harf takes a breather after a run on the Schuylkill River in Philadelphia. Harf's performance earned a gold medal in the eighth ESPN X Games wakeboarding competition held in August 2002.

Even during practice, Danny Harf exhibits the talent and style that enabled him to become a superstar in his sport. Harf slices through the wash on the Schuylkill River during a pre-competition run at the 2001 X Games VII in Philadelphia.

or a seasoned wakeboarder, looking at the sport through the eyes of one of its most accomplished riders may provide a new spin on familiar information.

Harf quickly became well known in the field because of the massive amount of talent he exhibited at a young age. His natural talents on the water combined with a smooth riding style helped him become a major force on the professional wakeboarding circuit. We'll take a look at what makes Harf tick, but we'll also take a peek behind the scenes and learn about the pressure of competition, the tournaments, the equipment, and the scores of things wakeboarders do to stay safe in the water.

Maybe you're a big fan of Harf's because you know he can ride like no one else, or maybe you've seen him rip extreme tricks and want to get to know the person behind the board. After all, Harf helped popularize wakeboarding, making it one of the coolest water sports around.

CHAPTER ONE
ENDLESS SUMMER

In order to understand what Danny Harf does so well, we first have to understand wakeboarding and the beach culture that created it. Several different sports have contributed to the evolution of wakeboarding, including two of the most popular and traditional water sports—surfing and waterskiing.

Surfing, a sport that has been popular in the United States since the 1960s, is considered the true granddaddy of wakeboarding. But surfing has had a much longer history. In western Polynesia, people have been riding the surf

Wakeboarding is a modern sport with ancient origins. In this illustration from 1875, Hawaiians surf off the coast of Honolulu.

using wooden boards for 3,000 years! In fact, much of what we know about surfing today comes from early European and Polynesian contact from the 1700s. Captain James Cook even wrote about seeing a pleasure-seeking Tahitian catch a long wave in an outrigger canoe. Surfing was also practiced in areas in South America around Peru and off the coast of western Africa.

Much of what makes contemporary surfing what it is today was developed in and around the Hawaiian Islands. Surfing is called *he`e nalu* in Hawaiian, or "wave

Duke Paoa Kahanamoku poses in his natural element, H_2O, in Los Angeles in August 1933. In addition to promoting the resurgence of modern surfing, Kahanamoku was a gold medalist in the 1912 and 1920 Olympic Games.

sliding," a practice closely tied to island traditions. Although few Hawaiians practiced surfing before the early 1900s, the pastime eventually increased in popularity thanks to some die-hard surfers and increased tourism. Early hard-core surfers included George Freeth and Duke Paoa Kahanamoku, sometimes called the father of modern surfing.

Thanks to Hawaii's booming tourist traffic in the 1950s, the popularity of surfing soared. It was about this same time that surfing spread to the mainland United States. Soon thousands of surfers, or "gremmies," found themselves jumping on boards along the Southern California coast. Before long, surfing became popular in movies, and a beach culture surrounding the sport made its mark on the industries of fashion, music, and art. To this day, surfing continues to influence American culture.

Surfing had been a common sport for beach dwellers for decades when wakeboarders finally appeared in the late 1980s. Surfers often tried early forms of the sport and rode the waves while being towed by boat. Offshoots of surfing, such as windsurfing, which uses a small sail attached to the board to gain momentum, soon began to appear. Another strange adaptation of surfing is called tow-in surfing. Tow-in surfing gives surfers exposure to bigger waves by towing the rider farther away from the shoreline on a Jet Ski. A Jet Ski is the water-based equivalent of a motorized scooter. Also in the late 1980s, a shorter surfboard evolved from the traditional long board.

The Evolution Begins

In 1985, Tony Finn, a surfer in San Diego, California, developed a smaller surfboard that he called a Skurfer. Riders using a Skurfer combined the techniques of surfing and waterskiing. The Skurfer riders were pulled from behind a boat as if they were waterskiing.

The Endless Summer

A true motion picture about surfing.
Filmed in Africa, Australia, New Zealand, Tahiti, Hawaii and California

A BRUCE BROWN FILM IN COLOR

Distributed by Cinema V

Later that summer, Finn and another surfing enthusiast, Jimmy Redmon, added foot straps to the Skurfer, which helped riders keep their feet in place. Redmon was working on his own version of a Skurfer called a ski board. Foot straps were very important to the eventual success of the wakeboard because they allowed riders to gain height, or "catch big air," while attempting tricks. Increased height helped riders develop new and more creative moves. By staying attached to the board, riders were able to perform a wider and more complicated range of movements without having to worry about losing the board from beneath them. In the beginning, only the strongest riders could perform deepwater starts on boards like Skurfers because other boards were more difficult to mount. Although Redmon's Skurfer was an improvement on the surfboard, it wasn't very durable.

As time passed, more people began experimenting with the new water sport that, at the time, was sometimes referred to as "skiboarding." As the sport gained attention, various groups and organizations began appearing. The World Wakeboard Association (WWA) was founded in 1989, and in 1990, the first Skurfer championships were televised.

Even with the popularity of skiboarding, the sport was still difficult for many riders to learn. This prompted skiboarding enthusiasts to develop better equipment. In the

Described as the definitive surf movie, the 1966 documentary *The Endless Summer* follows two surfers in their worldwide search for the perfect wave. The movie introduced the fledgling sport to a wider audience and contributed to its rise in popularity.

World Wakeboard Association

The WWA is the official organization in charge of officiating over wakeboarding worldwide. The WWA helps provide guidelines and consistent standards to be used for all professional wakeboarding events. The WWA reviews all major professional wakeboarding competitions, including the U.S. Pro Tour, the X Games, the U.S. Masters, Wakeboard U.S. Nationals, and Wakeboard Worlds.

WWA members are provided with the official WWA handbook, training information, and how-to guides for beginners who want to start contests and demos in their area.

1990s, the Hyperlite was invented by Herb O'Brien, which made wakeboarding easier and opened the doors to new riders. The Hyperlite was easier to ride because of its compression-molded material. Its buoyancy allowed riders to propel themselves out of the water more easily. Boards continued to be modified and improved, making way for more growth in the sport. In 1993, Redmon developed the twin-tip board. This design provided riders with even more versatility. Today's riders rely on the twin-tip design.

It was also during the 1990s that skiboarding and skurfing also became known as wakeboarding. In 1992, professional wakeboarding events became more popular, in part because they were being televised on cable stations such as ESPN. *Wake Boarding* magazine appeared that same year, and before long, there was a professional wakeboard tour sponsored by the WWA. Today, the ultimate titles for the professional wakeboarder are the Wakeboard World Cup and Vans Triple Crown of Wakeboarding.

Although Daniel Harf was born in Southern California, a place known for its turbulent surf, on October 15, 1984, he moved to the East Coast when he was a teenager. Harf's parents settled with Danny and his sister, Lauren, in Orlando, Florida, where water sports were and are a regular rite of passage. At thirteen years of age, he started wakeboarding.

Orlando provided convenient access to the ocean, which made learning the sport easier. Two years later, in 1999, Harf was already competing professionally and starting to make big waves in the world of wakeboarding. In 2000, he was considered the most promising rookie in the sport. By his sixteenth birthday, Harf had won the gold medal at the X Games VII.

Growing up in Orlando gave Harf access to some of the best wakeboarding resources. He and his friends were able to practice regularly. While the sport was still new in other parts of the United States, Florida was the home of many of the earliest and most talented wakeboarders throughout the 1990s. Pros like Shaun Murray and Darin Shapiro made it easy for Harf to find inspiration. Before long, Harf's older sister, Lauren, hit the surf with him. It should come as no surprise that Lauren quickly rose up the ranks of the professional world of wakeboarding and placed fifth in the 2001 X Games in Philadelphia, Pennsylvania.

"Daniel and I didn't get along when we were younger, but once he got to high school, that changed. It's funny because now we actually hang out with a lot of the same people. He has always been supportive of me in everything—not just in wakeboarding. He even skipped a tour stop just to go to my graduation. I thought that was really cool," said Lauren Harf in an interview with Wakelounge.com.

Danny Harf is an athlete who just seems to have what it takes to make it professionally. But he is more than just talented. For any professional athlete, being naturally gifted is only part of what is required for success. Dedication, a strong work ethic, a good attitude, and a little luck all play significant roles in Harf's overall achievements as an athlete.

As with any athletic career, the amount of practice an athlete gets is very important. Season schedules are grueling, and the competition is fierce. Because wakeboarding is still relatively new, professional riders are constantly pushing each other to develop more daring routines.

Under Pressure

Sometimes competitions can make even the most seasoned athlete crack under pressure. With all eyes on you, tension can make even the simplest trick seem impossible.

Harf set himself ahead of the pack with his incredible ability to recover after a bad spill. For example, in the men's professional wakeboard final in the 2002 X Games, Harf fell on one of his first tricks. Because he was defending the gold medal he had won the previous year,

Competition Highlights

1999 Wakeboard Nationals, Junior Men (second)
1999 Mountain Dew Pro, Junior Men's Champion
1999 Pro Wakeboard Tour, Atlanta, Junior Men's Champion
1999 U.S. Junior Series Champion
2000 Ford Ranger Wakeboarding Pro second
2000 Pro Wakeboard Tour, Detroit (third)
2000 Pro Wakeboard Tour, Oklahoma City, Champion
2000 Rookie of the Year
2001 X Games Champion
2002 U.S. Masters (third)
2002 Pro Wakeboard Tour, Orlando (third)
2002 Wakeboard Worlds (third)
2002 Gravity Games (second)
2002 X Games Champion
2003 X Games Champion

Danny Harf raises his board in triumph after winning gold in the 2002 ESPN X Games in Philadelphia.

Harf felt even more pressure to turn things around. He refocused and completed two great passes with a 720 and a 900 off the double-up to take home the gold for the second straight year. Harf threw in a whirlybird (a tantrum with a fully inverted 360 spin) and a KGB (a backside roll with a blindside 360). Harf followed with a Pete Rose (a frontside mobius with a grab), a Moby Dick (a tantrum with a blindside 360), and a backside boardslide.

Although Harf later said that he never expected to win, it was obvious to everyone that he didn't expect to lose, either. He pulled out all the stops to fight off Darin Shapiro and Shaun Murray for the gold. "I guess I don't let the pressure get to me," Harf said in an EXPN.com interview. "That's why I do so well here."

Training Day

Becoming a professional athlete may mean plenty of great things, but it certainly doesn't mean that you can stop practicing. Harf, like most athletes, spends a huge amount of time refining his skills. As a rider's ability increases, he or she will likely enter competitions that are more challenging. Emerging competitors and occasional injuries can become distracting and stop an unfocused rider from performing at his or her peak level.

To keep his edge, Harf spends a great deal of time perfecting older tricks as well as attempting new ones. "I ride four or five days of the week for one or two hours per day," Harf said in an EXPN.com interview. "It's hard on your body so I try to make when I ride count and not overdo it. I practice with Parks Bonifay, Shane Bonifay, and Erik Ruck."

Play It Safe

Injuries can end an athlete's professional career in the blink of an eye. Even a momentary loss of concentration by an athlete can lead to devastating results. "I threw out my knee about a month ago on a kicker," said Harf in an EXPN.com interview in 2002. "I [intentionally] missed the end of the Professional Tour and other events to save myself for the X Games. Then, my doctor said that I destroyed my ACL [anterior cruciate ligament], and I could make it worse by riding. So I try to take it easy when I'm practicing and really take it out in the competitions. After the season is over I'll go in and have surgery to repair the problem."

In order to keep healthy during the off-season, many riders will train long hours at a gym or practice other sports. Many wakeboarders also practice similar board-based sports such as snowboarding or skateboarding when it isn't practical to wakeboard. Others stick to a rigorous diet, regular stretching, and strength and endurance training in order to maintain or increase their edge from year to year.

If a rider is injured, difficult choices have to be made. Season-ending injuries mean that he or she has to make decisions about surgery and possibly altering their riding style. Sometimes riders have to permanently change the way they perform tricks to avoid reinjuring themselves. For example, knee injuries can be devastating to a wakeboarder if he or she cannot relearn his or her style of landing.

CHAPTER TWO
DANNY AND HIS CREW

Danny Harf hangs out with a number of professional riders and competes regularly with the best wakeboarders in the world. It's normal for athletes to build friendships with each other. Friends are a great source of inspiration and encouragement. Sharing improvement strategies and swapping ideas can help riders develop their routines.

What Makes a Good Wakeboarder?

Wakeboarders are renowned for their skill, strength, and high-speed reflexes. Most professional wakeboarders' bodies

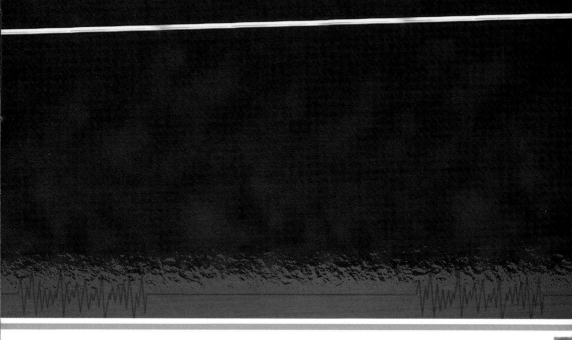

Darin Shapiro catches air at the 2002 ESPN X Games. Shapiro's ground-breaking moves push the envelope of professional wakeboarding.

• •

are slim and agile. These are just some of the reasons why so many young adults are drawn to wakeboarding.

Darin Shapiro has been a professional wakeboarder since 1991, and he has been a one-man wrecking ball. At five feet four inches tall (1.6 meters), Shapiro is living proof that the skills needed for professional wakeboard-ing run much deeper than stature.

Phillip "Froggy" Soven impressed everyone when he joined the Professional Wakeboarding Tour in 2001 at age eleven, the youngest in wakeboarding history. Like Harf,

Froggy is an up-and-coming competitor and proof that age is only a number.

To understand just how talented Harf is, let's examine some of his competitors. In this section, we'll discuss other wakeboarders, including some of Harf's closest friends.

Parks and Shane Bonifay

This brother duo from Lake Alfred, Florida, has been tearing it up professionally since the 1990s. Parks is a two-time X Games champion, a two-time national champion, and a three-time Pro Tour champion. Parks is almost a shoe-in when it comes to major competitions and has been a force to reckon with since 1996. Like Harf, Parks and Shane Bonifay are known for their crazy stunts and winning runs. Most of all, though, these Florida natives are all good friends. Even after Harf edged Parks out for the X Games gold in 2003, Parks was the first to congratulate Harf on the win.

Erik Ruck

Erik Ruck, another Florida resident and riding buddy of Harf's, has been a professional wakeboarder since 1998 and regularly placed in the top ten during his first season of competition. "We call Danny [Harf] 'Big Money,'" said Erik in an interview with EXPN.com. "He always seems to do well when there's a big purse up for grabs." Ruck was a 2002 and 2003 world wakeboard champion.

Shaun Murray

When someone establishes the first hall of fame for wakeboarding, chances are that Shaun Murray, a wakeboarder

Shaun Murray, a crowd favorite, takes a break at the August 2002 ESPN X Games in Philadelphia. His moves earned him third place in the wakeboarding competition.

from Orlando, will be its first inductee. Murray has placed regularly in the top ten since his first season of competition. Murray is a three-time world champion (1996, 1998, 2000), U.S. Masters champ (2001), Vans Triple Crown champion (2000), and a Pro Tour champion (1999).

Darin Shapiro

Darin Shapiro, who also hails from Orlando, has been involved with wakeboarding since 1991. He is noted for his

That's a Wrap!

Wakeboarding isn't the only thing Danny Harf is into these days. Harf and Shane Bonifay, along with other wakeboarders, are making a contribution to Hollywood with the company Pointless Productions. Throwing a new twist into the typical wakeboarding film, their film projects will be edgier with wilder tricks. The Pointless crew isn't only planning on taking over the wakeboarding film industry either. In the X Games IX in 2003, they dominated the finals, including winning the gold (Harf) and the silver (Bonifay). Harf's production company can be found online at www.pointlessproductions.com.

hard-nosed work ethic and well-mannered demeanor. Shapiro has won every title in the world of wakeboarding and has been largely responsible for inventing new tricks and pushing the sport to the next level. Shapiro's signature trick is the speedball. A speedball is a heelside double front flip, a highly difficult and dangerous maneuver. According to Tony Smith, an editor for *Alliance Wakeboard* magazine, "Darin is a legend when it comes to contest riding."

J. D. Webb

Harf knows what it's like to fight from the bottom up, so he likely sees some similarity between himself and the rise of another young rider, J. D. Webb. Webb, a sixteen-year-old wakeboarder from Polk City, Florida, won the Junior X title in 2003 by placing in five of the six tour stops. Keep an eye out for this competitor!

Female Wakeboarders

Harf and his buddies aren't Florida's only wakeboarding athletes. As with any sport, it's not surprising to see women stride through the ranks, as the strength, balance, and agility required for wakeboarding is making the sport popular with female athletes, too.

As wakeboarding's popularity grows with women, so do the resources and gear built for them. As more and more women became interested in wakeboarding, companies realized that they had to start meeting the demands of female riders. Today, there is plenty of gender-specific gear, including boards, bindings, boots, and gloves. Likewise, manufacturers in the wakeboarding world are quickly realizing the potential of female wakeboarders, and a number of professional teams now have female riders. Here's a profile of just some of the women leading the pack.

Dallas Friday

Dallas Friday has been a top competitor on the women's wakeboarding circuit ever since she became a professional competitor in 2000. Friday, another resident of Orlando, first picked up a wakeboard at age twelve, and within a year she was winning competitions and attracting sponsors.

Previously a gymnast, Friday has since pushed the world of women's wakeboarding over the top with complex moves that defy what was once considered normal competition. Although she suffered serious injuries in

May 2002, she has since rebounded and returned in top form. Friday recently shared the podium with Harf, when she won the gold in women's wakeboarding at the X Games IX in 2003. "It's pretty overwhelming to be sixteen [years old] and to be the best in the world," said Friday in an interview with ESPN after X Games IX. "I'm fortunate to be doing something that I love. This was the best X Games ever." Riders like Friday continually open the doors for other female riders and push the boundaries of what is expected on the women's pro wakeboarding circuit.

Tara Hamilton

Tara Hamilton, a wakeboarder from Lantana, Florida, took home the gold medal in the 2000 X Games and is known for her competitive spirit. Although she has also suffered injuries, she always comes right back and continually presses her female competitors to do even better. Hamilton took over the women's wakeboarding scene in 1997 by dominating the competition that year. She has since won the X Games twice (in 1997 and 2000) and has been a four-time WWA world wakeboard champion. "Tara [Hamilton] arrived at a time when women's wakeboarding needed a dominant performer,"

Dallas Friday prepares for her run in the final wakeboard competition at the 2003 ESPN X Games held in Long Beach, California. Like fellow Orlando native Danny Harf, Friday is a sport leader.

said Kevin Michael, managing editor of *Wake Boarding* magazine. "She stepped up the level of riding and served as inspiration for a new generation of lady rippers."

Emily Copeland

Emily Copeland, a wakeboarder from Denver, Colorado, has continually landed herself in the top of practically every event imaginable and recently finished third in the 2003 X Games IX behind Dallas Friday and Melissa Marquardt. Copeland has captured numerous titles since 1999, some of them twice. She has won the Vans Triple Crown, the U.S. Masters, the U.S. Open, the Pro Tour, and has even been a national and world wakeboarding champion.

A Word on Tony Hawk

While we're focused on people who have influenced wake-boarding, we have to mention Tony Hawk, the man largely responsible for the popularity of extreme sports. Even though he's not a wakeboarder, if you ask most of the pros what kind of an impact Hawk had on the whole X Games phenomenon, chances are you'll get a sense for the respect that people have for Hawk.

Hawk has been a one-man promotion for all extreme sports since he started competing in 1979. He has been a professional skateboarder for more than twenty years and has won thirteen medals in the X Games. Since he first began touring at the age of sixteen, Hawk has end-lessly promoted skateboarding and positively influenced the direction of many other related sports. Now married

Tony Hawk's achievements in the world of skateboarding and his dedication to the field of extreme sports have influenced a generation of wakeboarders. This move earned the Skateboard Vert Best Trick award at the X Games IX in Los Angeles in August 2003.

with three children, Hawk continues the promotion of extreme sports, including wakeboarding. For an inside look at Hawk's life on the road and what it really means to be a one-man traveling show, check out his book *Between Boardslides and Burnout*.

CHAPTER THREE
DANNY'S BAG OF TRICKS

A ll professional wakeboarders have a style that sets them apart from each other. Often this individuality is expressed as a certain consistency, a flair for the unusual, or a signature combination of tricks. This chapter will investigate Danny Harf's abilities and his gear as well as the different types of tricks and equipment of his competitors.

Harf is known for his smooth riding style and for performing difficult tricks like his backside Pete Rose. Generally, wakeboarding tricks are divided into five major

Harf performs an invert during the eighth annual ESPN X Games wakeboarding competition in Philadelphia in August 2002.

categories. Surface tricks are performed on the surface of the water. Grabs are performed while the rider is in the air, often directly leading into another move. Rotating the wakeboard and your body in the air results in what are generally referred to as spins. An invert, like a flip, is when a rider goes upside down. Raley-based tricks are performed on the raley, which means they are tricks performed with the rider's body extended back with the wakeboard above his or her head. Harf's favorite trick is the backside 180.

Trick List

Performing tricks with a wakeboard requires that riders understand a sequence of specific movements and the positions required for each. There are some great wakeboarding guides in publication that can actually guide you through each step in this process, often with pictures. Check out *Wake Boarding* magazine for other tips. The following is a list of tricks you'll undoubtedly hear mentioned during wakeboarding competitions or when reading about Harf or other professional wakeboarders.

air raley This trick is performed when a rider hits the wake and swings his or her board and body over his or her head as the wake is crossed. When performed correctly, the rider lands on the other side of the wake.

air roll A roll without using the wake.

backside roll Carving on the heelside edge, a rider brings the board up off the wake and over his or her head before landing facing the original direction. Harf is known for his backside moves.

butter slide Sliding the board sideways on top of the wake.

flip 'n' roll A flip is performed when the board tip goes over the tail, looking very similar to a cartwheel. Because the rider is standing sideways, sometimes a flip looks more like a roll to beginners. Likewise, a roll looks more like a flip or somersault. Remember that the term flip 'n' roll refers to the direction the board is moving, not the rider. In a roll, the rider rotates the board from heelside to toeside or vice versa.

frontside roll A toeside carve leading to rolling the board over the rider's head off the wake and landing on the other side of the wake.

grind Sliding the wakeboard along an obstacle in the water. Also known as a rail slide.

half-cab A fakie (backward) approach followed with a 180-degree rotation, crossing both wakes in the air. The rider lands in a forward position on the opposite side of the wake.

hoochie glide An air raley with a front-hand or heelside grab.

KGB A backside roll with a blind 360, employed by Harf in his 2002 X Games run.

method grab Crossing both wakes, the rider grabs the heelside edge of the board while "tweaking" his or her move (moving the board or legs while making the grab).

mobius A backside roll followed by a full twist.

Moby Dick A tantrum with a blindside 360; a signature Harf trick.

nose grab Grabbing the front tip of the board while airborne.

Pete Rose A frontside mobius with a heelside grab. Scott Byerly created the Pete Rose.

roast beef While flying over both wakes, the rider reaches an arm between his or her legs and grabs the heelside of the board.

scarecrow A front roll to fakie.

720 Two complete rotations with two handle passes. Harf used this trick to place first in the 2003 WWA championships.

speedball An advanced trick that includes two complete front flip rotations. The move was invented by Darin Shapiro.

tantrum A backflip over the wake.

temper tantrum Created by Parks Bonifay, this trick includes two tantrums before landing.

360 A spin in a complete circle while in the air.

whirlybird A tantrum with a fully inverted 360 spin. This trick wowed crowds during Harf's 2002 X Games performance.

Wakeboarding Tips

Everyone wants to learn how to make his or her jumps more spectacular and crowd-pleasing. Here are some hints on how you can get bigger air. First, make sure you accelerate all the way through the wake, not just on your carve. Second, when you reach the top of your wake, press off the board as if you're doing a little bunny hop. (Doing this will give you an added pop off the top of your jump.) Third, keep the tow rope tight until you are positioned at

A roast beef is just one of many awe-inspiring airborne moves developed by ambitious wakeboarders. While in midair, the rider reaches an arm between his or her legs and grabs the heelside of the board.

the top of your wake. This should maintain your acceleration through the jump. Finally, ask your fellow riders to review your best moves. Sometimes the jumps that are the cleanest don't always seem impressive to a beginner.

"Going out and throwing big technical tricks is very important [during competition]," Harf explained in an interview with EXPN.com. "You're riding with the top guys in the world. Any one of those guys in the final could win, so you've got to do something that makes you stand out against all those top riders, really try to go big and grab everything."

Everyone who wakeboards, whether beginner or professional, has his or her favorite equipment. When Harf's out on the water, he rides his own signature Hyperlite Premier 140 DNA with high-back boots. Harf signed with Hyperlite in 1999 and became the youngest rider to get his own pro model board. More recently, Harf won the X Games gold in 2003 on his new 2004 Hyperlite board.

Harf, like most professional wakeboarders, has a number of sponsors that assist him with some of the day-to-day costs of being a competitor. Whether by providing equipment, helping pay for travel costs, or promoting an athlete outside of events, sponsors are extremely important to professional athletes. Harf's sponsors include Hyperlite, Nautiques, Fox Racing, Billabong, Reef, Spy, and Performance.

While professional wakeboarders have the bonus of free gear, this can cause some unexpected problems for them. New equipment from various sponsors also means added responsibility for professional riders. As they decide to endorse one or more products, riders must also familiarize themselves with each new piece of equipment. For wakeboarders, the introduction of new equipment usually means having to adjust their riding style to accommodate different weights or altered positions. Even experienced professionals must adjust their riding style when they first use new equipment. New wakeboards are released all the time. A good way to find out about the latest release in equipment is to check out one of the many online board guides, such as the ones found on wakeboarder.com and wakelounge.com.

Wakeskating

If you've ever surfed or even skateboarded before, you might try wakeskating. In a simple sense, wakeskating is like wakeboarding without the bindings. Wakeskating is a nice alternative for beginners and advanced riders alike. From inventive new tricks and techniques to dock starts where riders make a timed run and jump, wakeskating lets creative wakeboarders attempt even more unbelievable stunts. "X Games has pushed the sport of wakeboarding and I can't wait until wakeskating is a part of it," said rider Brian Grubb in an interview with EXPN.com during the 2003 X Games.

Wakesurfing

Wakesurfing, a combination of wakeboarding and surfing, is also gaining in popularity. Wakesurfing actually predates wakeboarding. As a result of wakeboarding's increase in popularity, wakesurfing is also becoming well known.

A low-impact alternative to wakeboarding, wakesurfing uses the boat's wake as opposed to a natural wave. By

Communicating with Your Boat Driver

1. Thumb(s) up means go faster.
2. Thumb(s) down means go slower.
3. Pointing at an item of equipment means there is a problem with that item.
4. Pointing back toward an object means there is debris in the water.
5. Raising a hand overhead means a request for a re-ride.
6. A fallen rider must motion to the towboat or safety team to come back if he or she is injured and/or in danger.

riding close to the rear of the boat, a wakesurfer can coast easily behind the boat and practice tricks just as if he or she were surfing. Because of the close relationship between the boat and the rider, it is extremely important that wakesurfers use only an inboard boat. Wakesurfers should never use a boat with an outboard or inboard/outboard motor as its propeller can be dangerous. As with any water sport, riders should use a U.S. Coast Guard–approved life vest and follow all manufacturer recommendations for using the board and recommended weight for the board.

The Pull

Although wakeboarders get all the glory, they couldn't master a single trick without the pull, a wakeboarder's term for the boat that pulls you. Everyone has a tendency to take the boat driver for granted, whether he or she is a parent, friend, or another rider. But as any experienced wakeboarder will tell you, an attentive driver will make a good wakeboarding experience much better.

A good driver gets to know each rider and his or her routine, and all wakeboarders should know and understand the boat driver. Together, wakeboarders and boaters should agree upon an established speed and course. By paying attention to what each wakeboarder likes and trying his or her correct individual speed, the driver can ensure a safe and enjoyable time for everyone.

It's always a good idea to help share responsibilities on the water, no matter how small they might seem. Whether you're a third party or you periodically trade off driving the boat, make sure to help share duties like boat maintenance and cleaning and checking safety equipment. Doing so will help everyone have a good time.

The Double-Up

A popular wakeboarding trend known as the double-up is something that a good boat driver can help an experienced wakeboarder achieve. A double-up is created when the boat makes a full turn and passes back over its own original wake, creating a series of impressive waves. The boat driver must maintain a consistent speed through the double-up, which will also help provide the wakeboarder with more movement options. Harf has used this technique to his benefit, performing incredible 900s at the end of a run. Sometimes, using the double-up can help a wakeboarder solidify his or her lead and fight off the competition.

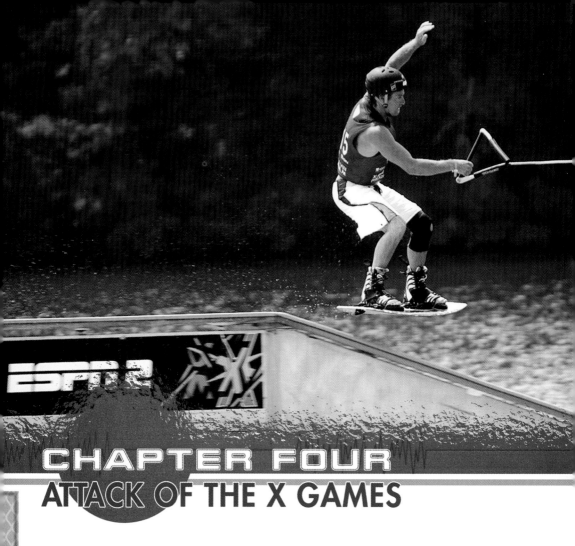

CHAPTER FOUR
ATTACK OF THE X GAMES

Professional wakeboarding would not be where it is today if it wasn't for the huge competitions and events that showcase its most talented and up-and-coming riders. Without the hype that the media world has extended to the sport, it never would have become so popular so quickly. Extreme sporting events also offer plenty of crossover opportunities to showcase similar sports. Sponsors believed, and it has since proved true, that most traditional fans of skateboarding or surfing are interested in wakeboarding, too. Fans of multiple sports may also share the same tastes in fashion

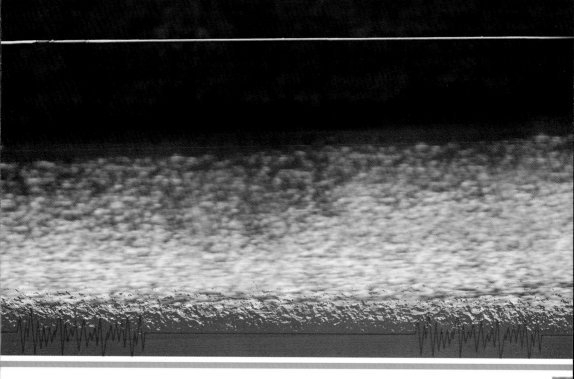

Danny Harf shown in midflight at the August 2002 X Games in Philadelphia. The X Games is the premier event in extreme sports.

• •

and music. In effect, many of the X Games competitions revolve around an entire youth culture that combines its interests in unique sporting events with demonstrations of new equipment, sports-related fashion, music, and, occasionally, political activism. For example, wakeboarding events are terrific venues to establish a greater interest in national environmental organizations such as Greenpeace, the Natural Resources Defense Council, or more regional organizations such as Clean Ocean Action in the Northeast. Attending the X Games will give any new wakeboarder a peek inside the extreme sport lifestyle. This chapter contains information about the types of events in which Danny Harf has appeared or might appear in the future.

The X Games

The Extreme Games—better known as the X Games—is the premier event for extreme sports. Established in 1995 out of a fascination with new and unusual sports, the X Games united a variety of common-minded athletes. The X Games challenged the old notion of traditional one-on-one or team sports and switched the focus to showcasing individual athletes.

The first X Games took place in Rhode Island and Vermont in 1995. More than 350 athletes competed in various events that included bicycle stunt riding, bungee jumping, street luge, skateboarding, mountain biking, windsurfing, and other similar events. Wakeboarding made its official debut in 1996, replacing kiteskiing, windsurfing, and mountain biking. Based on increasing attendance at the X Games, the first Winter X Games followed and included mountain bike racing over snow and shovel racing. Bungee jumping was retired as an event in 1997 and replaced with snowboarding. Within the span of a few years, other similar sporting events, such as the Asian X Games, the X Trials, and the X Games Road Show, also gained popularity.

Harf has swept the X Games recently by winning the gold in 2001, 2002, and 2003. Most recently, he won the X Games IX in Los Angeles, California, held at the Long Beach Marina. Harf kicked it off with a toeside nose-grab back roll to blind, setting the bar for the competition in what EXPN.com called "one of wakeboarding's best contest runs ever." Following his impressive start, Harf followed with a whirlybird 540 and a heelside 720, and he cemented his third X Games gold with a toeside slob 900 off the double.

The ninth annual X Games showcased more than 300 of the world's best action sports athletes in 2003. Most of the events were held at the Staples Center in Los Angeles, with other events staged at other surrounding venues. Today's X Games host a variety of competitions, including aggressive in-line skating, skateboarding, bike stunt riding, motocross (moto X), downhill BMX, surfing, and wakeboarding.

"I was pumped up to clinch my third gold medal," Harf said in an interview with EXPN.com in 2003. "There was a lot of pressure and expectation for me to win three in a row, plus my whole family was here cheering me on. [Winning X] opened up a lot of new doors and opportunities. It's made people respect my riding."

Harf has dominated the event three years in a row, but every athlete is raising the bar. When EXPN asked Harf about the competitive nature of wakeboarding, he commented, "Everybody seems amped to medal, so I'm expecting a lot of riders to step it up."

Junior X

Junior X is for younger riders and provides an exciting opportunity to become involved in the world of competitive wakeboarding. Following a similar format to the X Games, Junior X provides competitors under seventeen years of age

Standings

The following is a list of the latest top-ten standings for the Wakeboard World Cup.

2003 World Cup Standings

Men
1. Darin Shapiro
2. Brett Eisenhauer
3. Parks Bonifay
4. Josh Sanders
5. Daniel Watkins
6. Erik Ruck
7. Danny Harf
8. Shawn Watson
9. Shaun Murray
10. Shane Bonifay

Women
1. Dallas Friday
2. Emily Copeland
3. Maeghan Major
4. Lauren Loe
5. Tara Hamilton
6. Melissa Marquardt
7. Laura Lohrmann
8. Megan McNeil
9. Cheryl Newton
10. Lauren Harf

Parks Bonifay does a frontside board-slide at the 2003 Pro Wakeboard Tour competition in Detroit, Michigan.

(or eighteen for girls) with the opportunity to compete. Youngsters can test their skills on modified ramps and attend clinics and workshops with professional riders.

U.S. Pro Wakeboard Tour

The Pro Wakeboard Tour is a five-event circuit that runs throughout the riding season each year. It judges riders on a number of criteria, including the difficulty, variety, accuracy, and creativity of their routines. Judges also look for the feel of the ride or its fluidity. The overall score is determined from three categories:

33.3 Points—Execution This score reflects the level of technical difficulty of each maneuver performed, as well as the successful completion of the entire run with a minimum of falls.

33.4 Points—Intensity This score reflects the degree of performance in each maneuver performed in terms of how forceful the moves were, as well as the overall performance of the run.

33.3 Points—Composition This score reflects the overall composition of the run in terms of a rider's ability to perform a variety of maneuvers in a flowing, creative sequence.

Vans Triple Crown of Wakeboarding

The Vans Triple Crown features all kinds of extreme sports: skateboarding, BMX, freestyle motocross, surfing, snowboarding, and wakeboarding. In 2003, wakeboarding events were held in Texas, Indianapolis, Indiana, and Florida.

The Vans Triple Crown is really three separate events held throughout the year, made up of the Wakeboarding Pro, WWA Wakeboard Nationals, and the WWA Wakeboard World Championships.

Wakeboard World Cup

The Wakeboard World Cup is awarded to the rider who accumulates the best point total based on placement in a professional event. Professional events include those of the Pro Tour, the Vans Triple Crown, the X Games, and the Gravity Games. Winning the Wakeboard World Cup is an honor and signifies a rider who is consistently the best at what he or she does.

Gravity Games

A rival competition to the more widely attended X Games is the newer Gravity Games. The Gravity Games challenge the dominance of the X Games with the same event categories and a long list of sponsors and competitors. It's not surprising that other events that showcase extreme sports are beginning to catch on as the popularity of these sports reaches larger audiences.

Emily Copeland *(center)* celebrates her win at the September 2003 Gravity Games in Cleveland, Ohio. Tara Hamilton *(left)* took second place, followed by Leslie Kent *(right)*.

Harf performed well at the Gravity Games 2002, grabbing the silver medal. Consistent with his style, he recovered from a fall during his first pass and nailed his second with a tootsie (a front-roll blind 180) roll, a Moby Dick, and a method-to-scarecrow (grabbing the heel edge of the board before making a toeslide front roll with a 180 degree turn). Just to really put the digs in his competition, he launched the first good crowd-pleasing double-up of the day at the end of his sequence, a 900.

The U.S. Masters

The U.S. Masters is the longest-running and most prestigious water sports tournament in the world. A handful of athletes are selected each year to compete in the Masters for one of the largest cash prizes awarded in the field of water sports.

The U.S. Masters is an invitation-only event held annually over Memorial Day weekend. It has been instrumental in popularizing new varieties of water sports. Before wakeboarding was as well known as it is today, the U.S. Masters helped increase people's knowledge and respect for the fledgling sport. In 1994, wakeboarding was added to the U.S. Masters as an official event.

Competition Day

Harf is known to both his competitors and fans alike as a person who is cool under pressure. But what is competition day really like for Harf or for any professional wakeboarder for that matter? Besides getting your gear ready and preparing yourself mentally, competitions are generally a time for athletes to get together to support one another as well as to compete. "Every week is different; sometimes you feel it and sometimes you don't, whether it's competing or having fun. I've learned to balance what's important to me," said Harf in an interview with EXPN.com.

Preparations will vary somewhat depending on the event, but in general, each competitor will get several attempts to showcase his or her best tricks. The Gravity Games allow each wakeboarder one run in the final test. Each rider gets a first pass at the course, which is complete with A-frame sliders and launch ramps. After the rider's first pass, there is a 30-second break, which gives the water enough time to settle down before the rider makes a second pass through the course. This second run is in the opposite direction. Finally, each competitor gets a single double-up hit at the end of the run.

CHAPTER FIVE
RIDE LIKE THE WIND

Although wakeboarding is a difficult sport for beginners, many young people are interested in trying it. Every beginner should first learn how to swim. Next, get familiar with the basics of wakeboarding and its safety requirements. Begin by trying related sports such as waterskiing, skateboarding, or snowboarding, which might be a little easier for first-time riders. Whichever water sport you decide to try, remember to wear a U.S. Coast Guard–approved life vest and listen to the rules set down by your boat driver.

Wakeboarding combines the skills of several sports. Many people first get their feet wet with waterskiing, skateboarding, or snowboarding.

First Foot First

The first thing to do when learning how to wakeboard is to figure out how you would like to stand on the board. Which foot would you feel comfortable placing forward? If you have skateboarded or snowboarded before, chances are very good that you'll prefer the same foot forward.

To help you decide, simply stand with both feet together, look straight ahead, and ask a friend to give you a slight push from behind. (The push should be just enough to make you step forward one step with either foot.) As with all of us, you will favor one foot for stability over another. This foot will become your "foot forward" and will likely feel the most natural to you. If you prefer to ride with your left foot forward, this position is referred to as "normal." If you instead prefer your right foot forward, this position is referred to as "switchstance," "goofy," or "fakie." Generally, right-handed people ride "normal," and left-handed people ride "goofy," but this is not always the case.

Normally, wakeboarders' preferences depend on how they like to ride. It's always a good idea to try both positions when you're starting, just to see if you feel more comfortable with one over the other. Advanced riders sometimes learn how to ride both ways.

The Wakeboard

If you're serious enough about wakeboarding to purchase your own wakeboard, research the wide range of equipment available for you. If you're lucky enough to have hand-me-down equipment, this is a good start. Most riders generally won't have equipment preferences until they've tested a number of options.

Numerous wakeboarding publications and Web sites provide annual equipment guides that are a great source for information on the latest boards and gear. Some guides

Finding the appropriate board involves many decisions, from the length and width of the board and the size of the bindings to which designs match a wakeboarder's personal style.

provide additional information on which boards are better for beginning riders. They also point out which might be good transitional boards and others that are specifically built for a more advanced riding style.

Buying Danny Harf's signature Hyperlite board may impress your friends, but they'll be more impressed if you're willing to get out there and shred, regardless of what you're riding. Consider buying an older model board. Not only will you save money, but you also won't be completely dissatisfied if you have to switch to a more accommodating board later.

Bindings

Sometimes the easiest way to pick the correct bindings is simply to test the board with various settings to see which one feels the most comfortable. Most intermediate and advanced riders will often prefer a kind of duck-footed binding setting. This is one that sets your leading foot and trailing foot pointed slightly to the front and back of the board, respectively. If you set your bindings in this way, you can ride with alternate feet forward.

Although a duck-footed binding setting will allow more options for riders, most beginners prefer setting their bindings with either the right or left foot facing forward. This means setting the trailing foot on the board with the front foot turned outward. Beginners have a tendency to lean over the top of their board. Setting the bindings back from the board's center will help to compensate for this situation.

Sometimes bindings can be very difficult to get into, especially when they are new or when you're putting them on dry. Dunking the bindings in water or using a "slime" that you can pick up at your local wakeboarding shop can help you ease your foot into position. Remember that it's generally a good thing to make sure your bindings are snug, but they shouldn't be cutting off or slowing blood circulation to your feet. At the same time, slipping too easily in and out of bindings while riding can lead to injury. If you think the bindings might be too small, take your board in to your local shop and ask for an expert fitting and advice.

Fins

Fins on a wakeboard will assist the wakeboarder by adding varying amounts of control and stability, depending on his or her needs. Most beginners prefer longer fins, while shorter fins will allow for more advanced tricks that release the board from the water. Longer fins are helpful for buoyancy when learning how to get up onto the board as well as for basic riding. As a rider advances and begins learning various tricks and moves that require increased flexibility, he or she will need to switch to smaller fins.

Wakeboarding Fans Agree

Danny Harf is a wakeboarding favorite because of his good attitude and sportsmanship. In fact, in the October 2003 issue of *Wake Boarding* magazine, Harf was voted number four in the magazine's annual survey of favorite riders.

Danny Harf's groundbreaking moves and good attitude make him a favorite among wakeboarding pros and fans. Danny celebrates with the fans after winning the wakeboarding competition at the 2002 X Games in Philadelphia, Pennsylvania.

Other fans of the sport appreciate Harf's unique riding style and his ability to continually push the envelope with new moves. "Just coming up with something new and doing [tricks] I haven't done before [motivates me to ride]," he said in a 2003 *Wake Boarding* interview. No matter what the future holds for Harf, his fans can be sure to see him competing for gold at the eleventh annual X Games in 2005.

air roll   A roll that doesn't use the wake for any lift.

backside   The backside of the board, where the wake-boarders heels rest; also referred to as heelside.

bindings   The straps or booties that hold a rider's feet in place on top of the wakeboard.

blind   Generally refers to a wakeboarder who can't see either the boat or the wake.

boardslide   A rail slide with the wakeboard perpendicular to the rail, which is the curved bottom part of a wakeboard.

boat speed   The ideal boat speed for a wakeboarder is between 18 and 22 miles per hour (29 to 35 kilometers per hour). The speed should be fast enough to keep the board skimming on top of the water and to make a good wake for jumping.

butter slide   A slide along the edge of the wake.

dock start   When a rider starts in a seated or standing position on a dock. The boat pulls the rider off the dock and into the water.

double-up   Refers to a large wake that is created when a boat does a wide turn and crosses its own wake.

fakie   Backward also known as a switchstance position. For goofy-footers, this means riding with the left foot forward. For regular-footers, it's riding with the right foot forward.

frontside   The front side of the wakeboard, where the wakeboarders toes rest; also known as toeside.

goofy-footers   Riders who prefer to ride with their right foot forward.

handle pass   The switching of the handle from one hand to the other while spinning.

heelside   The backside of the board, where the wakeboarder's heels rest.

helmet   Required equipment for certain tricks and competitions; it helps to protect the wakeboarder's head from injury during a collision.

invert   A trick in which a wakeboarder moves off of the wake and the board gets higher than the rider.

kicker   A curved ramp that launches the wakeboarder, similar to a quarter-pipe.

nose   The tip of the wakeboard.

Skurfer   An early wakeboard, which was narrower, without bindings, and more buoyant.

360   A full rotation complete with a handle pass or wrapping the rope around the body.

toeside   The front edge of the board, where a wakeboarder's toes rest.

towrope   A rope attached to the back of the boat. The wakeboarder holds on to a handle at the other end of the rope.

tweak   Adding a little extra flair to a trick or move by twisting the body.

wake   A wavy trail that a boat leaves behind itself as it moves through the water.

Pro Wakeboard Tour
World Sports & Marketing
460 N. Orlando Avenue, Suite 200
Winter Park, FL 32789
(407) 628-4802
Web site: http://www.prowakeboardtour.com

World Wakeboard Association (WWA)
P.O. Box 1964
Auburndale, FL 33823
(863) 551-1683
Web site: http://www.thewwa.com

Eight colleges across the United States currently offer various levels of financial aid and scholarships for water-skiers. These include Alabama State University, Arizona State University, Eckerd College, Florida Southern College, Florida Gulf Coast, Rollins College, University of Louisiana at Lafayette, and University of Louisiana at Monroe. If you're interested in finding out more about available scholarships or financial aid, start by filling out the National Collegiate Recruitment Database form found at http://www.ncwsa.com.

Web Sites

Due to the changing nature of Internet links, the Rosen Publishing Group, Inc., has developed an online list of Web sites related to the subject of this book. This site is updated regularly. Please use this link to access the list:

http://www.rosenlinks.com/exb/dhar

FOR FURTHER READING

Baccigaluppi, John, Sonny Mayugba, and Chris Carnel. *Declaration of Independents: Snowboarding, Skateboarding and Music: An Intersection of Cultures.* San Francisco: Chronicle Books, 2001.

Gaines, Ann Graham. *The Composite Guide to Extreme Sports.* Philadelphia: Chelsea House Publishers, 2000.

Hawk, Tony. *Between Boardslides and Burnout.* New York: HarperCollins Publishers, 2002.

Koeppel, Dan. *Extreme Sports Almanac.* Lincolnwood, IL: Lowell House, 2000.

Wampler, Patrick. "Harf & Copeland take X Games VIII." EXPN.com. Retrieved October 30, 2003 (http://expn.go.com/xgames/sxg/viii/archive/).

Wampler, Patrick. "Q & A with Danny Harf." EXPN.com. Retrieved October 30, 2003 (http://expn.go.com/xgames/sxg/viii/s/QA_dannyharf.html).

Wimmer, Dick ed. *The Extreme Game.* Short Hills, NJ: Burford Books, 2001.

Magazine

Wake Boarding
330 West Canton Avenue
Winter Park, FL 32792
Web site: http://www.wakeboardingmag.com

BIBLIOGRAPHY

Baccigaluppi, John, Sonny Mayugba, and Chris Carnel. *Declaration of Independents: Snowboarding, Skateboarding and Music: An Intersection of Cultures.* San Fransisco, CA: Chronicle Books, 2001.

Gaines, Ann Graham. *The Composite Guide to Extreme Sports.* Philadelphia: Chelsea House Publishers, 2000.

Hawk, Tony. *Between Boardslides and Burnout.* New York: HarperCollins Publishers, 2002.

Hayhurst, Chris. *Wakeboarding! Throw a Tantrum.* New York: The Rosen Publishing Group, Inc., 2000.

Koeppel, Dan. *Extreme Sports Almanac.* Lincolnwood, IL: Lowell House, 2000.

McKenna, Anne T. *Extreme Wakeboarding.* Mankato, MN: Capstone Press, 2000.

Wimmer, Dick, ed. *The Extreme Game.* Short Hills, NJ: Burford Books, 2001.

INDEX

About the Author

Christopher Goranson lives in Denver, Colorado, with his wife Lindsay. Christopher spends his summers waterskiing in Clear Lake, Iowa, and winters skiing and snowboarding throughout Colorado's high country. You can contact him at wakeboarding@row14.com.

Photo Credits

Front cover (left), pp. 1, 4, 17, 23, 40–41, 56 © Tony Donaldson/Icon Sports Media; front cover (right), p. 12 © Swin Ink/Corbis; pp. 26, 44, 47 © Mike Isler/Icon Sports Media; back cover image © Nelson Sá; pp. 6, 20–21, 30–31 © Icon Sports Media; pp. 8–9 © Culver Pictures, Inc.; p. 10 © AP/World Wide Photos; p. 29 © Matt A. Brown/Corbis; pp. 34, 53 © Tony Donaldson/Icon Sports Media/Rosen Publishing; pp. 50–51 © Murry Sill/IndexStock.

Designer: Nelson Sá; **Editor:** Joann Jovinelly;
Photo Researcher: Peter Tomlinson